VOGUE ON

DOLCE & GABBANA

Luke Leitch & Ben Evans

Hardie Grant

QUADRILLE

Domenico Dolce and Stefano Gabbana take to a classic Italian moped for Vogue in 1997. Photograph by Julian Broad.

Page 1 *Dolce & Gabbana's passions – tradition, craftsmanship, femininity, sensuality and subversion – exemplified in an intricately embroidered mesh corset from their autumn/winter 1997 collection.*

Previous page *Patrick Demarchelier photographs Agyness Deyn in a saturated rose-print silk bustier and pencil skirt from autumn/winter 2011.*

'DREAMS CAN STILL COME TRUE;
YOU NEED A GREAT DEAL OF
ENERGY AND DETERMINATION,
AND A LITTLE BIT OF LUCK.'

STEFANO GABBANA

MAKING IT BIG

It has taken three decades for designers Domenico Dolce and Stefano Gabbana to grow their two-man start-up run from a tiny studio into a multi-billion-dollar international fashion superbrand. The progress of Dolce & Gabbana can be traced through the hundreds of pages of sumptuous editorial photography the house has inspired in *Vogue*, but the story begins in Milan.

Today, Silicon Valley is to technology what Milan was once to fashion. From the mid-1970s through to the mid-1980s the capital of Lombardy was at the heart of a 'Made in Italy' ready-to-wear revolution, a happy meeting of circumstance and opportunity in which a select group of trailblazing talents built businesses that would become famous across the globe. *Stilisti*, or designers, such as Albini, Armani, Krizia, Fiorucci, Ferré, Missoni, Moschino and Versace joined the Old Masters – Fendi, Prada, Gucci – in becoming household names. Milan proved the perfect crucible for this great post-couture fashion democratisation, eclipsing Florence and Rome. This was thanks to an intertwining of artisanal ingenuity, manufacturing know-how, progressive retailing strategies promoted by department stores like La Rinascente and an atmosphere of intellectual creativity that had, hitherto, been focused on art, architecture and furniture design; these were all combined with entrepreneurial aspiration.

A recurring motif of the design house – roses – here come scattered across brocade on an off-the-shoulder, tightly-bodiced minidress worn by model Georgia May Jagger and photographed by Mario Testino, April 2015.

It was in Milan that Domenico Dolce and Stefano Gabbana first made contact in 1981 aged twenty-three and nineteen respectively. Gabbana, who had grown up in Milan and had briefly studied graphic design there, decided he wanted to work in fashion, Milan's most dynamic industry. He had heard that there might be a position available in the studio of the designer Giorgio Correggiari, and phoned up to try his luck. Dolce, who was Correggiari's first assistant, answered and – in a slightly unorthodox fashion – arranged to meet the candidate in a nightclub named No Ties, where Correggiari's team was due to throw a party for the British band Imagination. On the night they first met,

Gabbana might well have thought he was hallucinating, for Dolce was dressed as a priest – a clubbing outfit that neatly anticipated the ironic (and iconic) sacrilege that would become a key theme for them both.

The interview went well and Gabbana joined Correggiari's team. For eighteen months they both continued to work there, leaving to embark on a working relationship and to establish a blossoming romantic one. Together they moved into an affordable but tiny two-room office, from which they freelanced for companies including MaxMara and Marzotto. They phoned Giorgio Armani in the hope of work in Milan's top fashion house but were never called back.

In a moody scene of domestic neorealism photographed by Karim Sadli in 2015, model Damaris Goddrie embodies a modern-day Anna Magnani – the star of Italian Neorealist cinema and an important inspiration for Dolce & Gabbana – in the designers' black crêpe dress under a wool polo-neck.

Then they tried their hand at producing a line of their own, called *Donna, Donna* (a name Dolce had originally coined under advice from Corregiari as a play on his own initials). This received enough positive reaction from the press and buyers for the young team to approach a factory about putting it into production, a deal that then mysteriously fell through. Years later, they discovered that the factory was dissuaded from accepting the proposal by the influential commercial manager for an established label, who had cruelly dismissed them to the manufacturer as 'donkeys'. The snub, and the setback, still rankle (particularly with Gabbana) even thirty wildly successful years later.

'The Dolce & Gabbana woman has a life that reaches beyond, complete with fantasy, turmoil and always a story.'

VOGUE

Unnerved but undeterred, for a while they sold experimental, no-label designs to a number of Milan boutiques. Then in October 1985 opportunity knocked. Beppe Modenese, the curatorial dynamo who in 1977 had first unified the city's emerging designers under the umbrella of a tightly organised Milan fashion week, had become aware that his schedule was now so congested with established names – names he had been partly responsible for fostering – that younger designers and new ideas were finding themselves marginalised.

As Bernadine Morris reported in *The New York Times*, Modenese promised to 'give young people a chance and to give an idea of what's coming next in fashion'. By polling Milan's buyers and journalists for a list of their favourite fashion start-ups he would select three labels to present a collection. Dolce and Gabbana made the list. 'We cried', Gabbana recalled later of the moment Modenese offered them a chance to show. 'It was like getting to the Olympics. You see the calendar and it says Giorgio Armani, Gianni Versace, Gianfranco Ferré …'

The designers had three months and savings of just two million lire (about £850) with which to design and produce their first runway collection, which was cut by Gabbana to Dolce's sketches. They also had to choose a name for their label: they consulted the tag by their doorbell, which read *Dolce & Gabbana*.

On a sketch for the autumn/winter 1997 collection inspired by Fellini's epic Roma, swatches of tiger- and leopard-print chiffon indicate both the whimsy and ferocity to be brought to the elegant and sensuous lines of a structured sheath dress.

Overleaf *Shot by Regan Cameron, model Elsa Benítez projects all the sultry heat of the Dolce & Gabbana woman in an exotic leaf-print chiffon slip dress from the spring/summer 1997 collection.*

'Dolce does almost all of the tailoring, first sketching the outfits, and then slowly building up prototypes in muslin, on dozens of mannequins around his studio. Gabbana helps with selecting the fabric and deciding on the over-all feeling of a collection.'

THE NEW YORKER

'WE MAKE
CLOTHES THAT
MAKE YOU
FEEL, MAKE
YOU DREAM AN
ITALIAN DREAM.'

DOMENICO DOLCE

An audience of over 600 saw that first collection, which was christened *Geometrissimo*. Morris characterised the collection as 'clothes with a Japanese flavour … far freer than those shown by the established houses'. This was praise indeed, making reference to the wave of Japanese designers including Rei Kawakubo and Yohji Yamamoto who had conquered Paris in the early part of the decade with their softer, sculptural lines and abstract shaping. As Dolce told *Vogue* in 2005, 'Power-dressing dominated the scene. We wanted to go ahead of the trend and create something new, linear and stretchy.' The collection was notable for its multifunctionality, or as *Vogue Italia* coined it upon later reflection, *pluriportabilità*. Unpadded, slinky clothing could be worn either way up, or with two holes through which to place a head, emphasising the sensual slouch of a garment, and giving a taste of the body-focused direction of their future design.

Stretchy materials and linear, body-focused outlines continued to feature in Dolce & Gabbana designs: here Dewey Nicks pictures a diamanté-trimmed powder-blue party dress and matching sandals in 1995.

As with *Donna, Donna*, Dolce & Gabbana's first ever collection received positive reviews. And, as before, the designers found a manufacturer that initially agreed to produce it for retailers – but which then mysteriously reneged on that agreement. The two twenty-somethings searched frantically for a substitute factory, but failed and sent a letter cancelling their fabric order. In high dudgeon they retired to Polizzi Generosa, the small Sicilian town in which Dolce was born and raised, to spend Christmas with his family. There they found salvation. Dolce's parents ran a tailoring and haberdashery business, which in the 1970s his father had grown into a small menswear factory. It was his brother-in-law, Dolce later recalled, who made the crucial suggestion: 'Why doesn't the family try to make your clothes?' A serendipitous postal strike meant that the letter cancelling their fabric order hadn't yet reached its destination. They were on.

Geometrissimo was followed up by a collection that made a virtue of Dolce & Gabbana's poverty. *Real Women* included outerwear made of cotton jersey and denim, which the designers rubbed with pumice stones to achieve a distressed, worn look. Gabbana later recalled: 'We didn't even have money to buy shoes or accessories. So I asked my

friends to borrow things, from Manolo Blahnik, Moschino, Ferré, so it would be like how a woman uses things from lots of designers in ordinary life. I bought clocks in vintage shops to make jewellery. Some necklaces were made from ceramic equipment that's used on electricity poles.' In what was their first solo show, the collection was modelled by friends and volunteers on a catwalk separated from backstage by the designers' own bedsheets.

I t was their third collection, spring/summer 1987's *Trasformismo*, that first gave observers a real signal that Dolce & Gabbana might be a label on the rise. The buyers and editors in the audience for the designers' 9am show (held in their tiny, fifth floor showroom) saw *pluriportabilità* dresses and t-shirts in a range of innovative new fabrics. These included a stretch crêpe developed by Dolce & Gabbana in collaboration with a small factory in Como and a transparent double organza jersey. Velcro panels allowed the garments to be worn in multiple ways, and everything was reversible and re-shapable. It was with *Trasformismo* that Dolce & Gabbana really captured *Vogue*. First embraced, naturally, by their home edition, the pair featured in a short profile with a portrait by Renato Grignaschi in the January 1987 issue of *Vogue Italia*. The magazine praised the 105-piece collection of garments that were 'different from each other but linked to one another, with, at its core, a corollary of simple pieces to combine with them: T-shirts, jackets, skirts'. A collection, it agreed, for 'real women'. The collection also represented Dolce & Gabbana's first commercial success internationally, as it was bought by Browns in London (who had ignited John Galliano's career and brought Comme des Garçons and Calvin Klein to London) and Charivari in New York, also known for its introduction of emerging Italian and Japanese talents.

The autumn/winter 1987 collection brought Dolce & Gabbana to the pages of British *Vogue*, which explained the label's emergence in the September issue within a context of new Italian romance and sensuality, spearheaded by the likes of Romeo Gigli. The report praised

A 24-year-old Stefano Gabbana and a 28-year-old Domenico Dolce pose for a portrait by Michel Arnaud as Vogue *celebrates their being at the forefront of young Milanese fashion talent at the autumn/winter 1987 collections. Citing them as key players in 'Milan's feminine renaissance', Dolce & Gabbana are praised for their 'soft lines and mellifluous palette'.*

the pair's agent- and assistant-free approach to design, their unique fabric experiments and a mastery of colour, pairing various subdued earthy colours with black. The 'real woman' was again cited as a focus for the pair, who were quoted as saying 'We want to design for the softer more feminine woman, with the looks of actress Anna Magnani'.

This was a watershed collection for another reason. Dolce, who had been in creative thrall to the minimalism of Japanese design, was now persuaded by Gabbana to embrace his roots. Thus the collection, entitled *La Sicilia* and later described by Dolce as '*romantico* but never *aggressivo*', gently incorporated key themes drawn from the island of his birth, most particularly the flash of white shirt worn under a sensuous but austere black dress. It took Gabbana's outsider's eye to realise the rich potential of Sicilian iconography, and Dolce's intimate knowledge to express it fully.

Yasmin Le Bon smoulders in several layers of texture by Dolce & Gabbana, shot by Hans Feurer in 1988. The sensuality of the label was already established, and here a relatively conservative skirt length and a chiffon shirt exposing just a slight triangle of torso both help to fashion a wholly seductive ensemble.

To advertise the collection, the designers recruited the Sicilian reportage photographer Ferdinando Scianna. Marpessa Hennink, the Dutch-Surinamese model, agreed to model for free. Together the four of them set off around Sicily to shoot. 'He used just one camera and we shot for two or three days going off in a car', Gabbana later recalled, 'and we used the headlights for the light source'. Scianna said of the shoot: 'Through their clothes and Marpessa who wore them I attempted to take a journey with the memory of my Sicilian childhood.' The resulting pictures were beautiful evocations of Sicily's rough romance in which Marpessa, unmade-up, hair loosely back, and shot in black and white, looked simultaneously raw and ravishing.

It was next season, spring/summer 1988, that won Dolce & Gabbana its first full editorial page in *Vogue*. Shot by Hans Feurer, the black jacket, tea rose-coloured half-buttoned shirt and loosely abundant layered black chiffon skirt modelled by Yasmin Le Bon was a neat encapsulation of a collection that took the Sicilian theme from the season before and ran with it. Entitled *Il Gattopardo*, the collection drew inspiration from Italian Neorealist director Luchino

Visconti's 1963 film *The Leopard* (*Il Gattopardo*), an adaptation of Giuseppe Tomasi di Lampedusa's poignant account of Sicilian aristocracy's decline. *The Leopard*'s sumptuous nostalgia has become a cornerstone reference for Dolce & Gabbana, and in this collection they contrasted baroque full skirts with their first ever corsetry-as-outwear looks as well as the incorporation of brocade and seemingly priestly (but backless) white shirts.

As if having found the soul with which to underpin their technical skill and perfected the nuances of a working relationship, for the next two seasons the designers continued to refine their Sicilian-infused metier. They incorporated masculine tailoring for the first time in the autumn/winter 1988 *Baroque-Neorealism* collection, which was again heavily influenced by Visconti. And in spring/summer 1989 they presented their first corset dress and the first pieces made entirely in crochet. Dolce later said, 'by the end of this season, the whole world had a clear idea of what Dolce & Gabbana [was] about'. Furthermore, that idea was making a profound impression. As Liz Tilberis, editor in chief of *Vogue* between 1987 and 1992, wrote of Dolce & Gabbana: 'It's the first show on the schedule and always has a buzz about it, like the beginning of a term. The remarkable thing is, 500 collections later at the end of term you always remember what their show was like – which is one very good indicant of the mark they are making on the fashion consciousness.'

A very feminine expression of Dolce & Gabbana's masculine tailoring: Nadja Auermann poses in a marshmallow-pink wool three-piece suit from the spring/summer 1992 La Dolce Vita collection. The supermodel is even provided with a carriage for a Chinese Crested dog in the form of the designers' gilt, bead and cameo-laden evening bag. Photograph by Eric Boman.

'Style is personality.
It's the ability to look at things
beyond fashion and the self-confidence
to transform even the simplest thing
into something special.'

DOLCE & GABBANA

By the start of the 1990s, Dolce & Gabbana had established a foothold in Milan's fiercely competitive fashion system, and made a lasting impression on fashion internationally. They would start the decade with the launch of a menswear line, extending their reach into new boutiques and wardrobes as well as the 'Men in *Vogue*' pages of the magazine. The label was given its first British *Vogue* cover in August 1992. Shortly after the release of *Thelma & Louise*, Peggy Sirota pictured the film's co-star Geena Davis, arms flung out in a black lace body and perched upon a leopard-print pouffe. Dolce & Gabbana had now captured both *Vogue* and Hollywood, a potent combination.

Meanwhile, Dolce and Gabbana were rapidly building their business by opening stand-alone stores. By 1992 they had two in Milan, and one each in Tokyo and Hong Kong, as well as 350 wholesale accounts and a turnover of over $62 million, all the while securing lucrative sideline deals that reflected how fast their brand – and recognition of it – had grown. In 1992 *Vogue* noted the debut fragrance (called simply 'Dolce & Gabbana'), and later spoke to Dolce about the challenges – and rewards – of diversifying into perfume. He said: 'To get a scent that lasts is every designer's dream. It's not just that your business enters another sphere, but that you have the financial flexibility to be freer in your fashion collections.'

Dolce & Gabbana's ascent fitted perfectly into the 1990s' renewed love affair between fashion and Hollywood. With more and more stars featuring on the front of Vogue, Dolce & Gabbana's brand of flattering, feminine and forthright fashion became the preferred choice. Here Geena Davis appears on the cover of the August 1992 issue in a photograph by Peggy Sirota.

'We think of how a woman will feel in our dresses. Will she feel beautiful? Will she feel sexy?'

DOLCE & GABBANA

VOGUE

£2.30

**GEENA
DAVIS**
in a league
of her own

Catwalk talk

**What you need to know
from the new collections**

BEAUTY
how to look like a girl
when you dress like a man

In autumn 1993, Dolce and Gabbana signed a six-year partnership deal with manufacturer Ittierre S.p.A. to produce a diffusion line named D&G. The designers were already designing a second collection under contract to Complice (a successful and widely-distributed label owned by Italian manufacturing giant Genny), but D&G quickly eclipsed it and the Complice arrangement ended in 1994. Although this initialled second offering (a combination of sportswear and interpretations of vintage clothing for which the designers had noticed a renewed fervour among the youngsters of grunge) was featured far less often than the main line within the pages of *Vogue*, it gave the company a financial stability on which to push on for yet more growth, as well as a hugely powerful marketing tool in the form of its logo in distinctive sans-serif type.

Dolce & Gabbana's parallel work for Italian label Complice paved the way for the launch of their own secondary line, D&G. A serene Vanessa Duve, photographed by Albert Watson in 1993, models a Complice organza shirt whipped into corsages at the shoulder, with a woollen waistcoat and leggings, and set off by a military sash.

1994 saw the launch of their first men's fragrance, Pour Homme, as well as a new home collection based on treasures the pair had sourced from travels around the world. Fitting into what *Vogue* described as 'a new Arts and Crafts movement for the stay-at-home nineties', it featured bright majolica earthenware and soft furnishings upholstered in patchworked lace, velvet and antique tapestry. Patchwork, a new Dolce & Gabbana favourite, perfectly reflected their increasingly magpie-like tastes: 'We like [it] immensely, since it gathers different experiences and inspirations', they explained.

In 1995, a year in which Kate Moss appeared on the cover of *Vogue*'s October issue in a D&G micro-skirt, the magazine illustrated a feature in its May issue on the glorious rise of the supermodel with a Snakes & Ladders game that charted twelve steps to making the grade. The twelfth step, naturally, was bagging your first *Vogue* cover, but the penultimate was appearing on the catwalk of Dolce & Gabbana.

By the mid-Nineties the Dolce & Gabbana woman had fully arrived, and was growing both more confident yet still retaining a mysterious allure. *Vogue* characterised her as having 'a life that reaches beyond, complete with fantasy, turmoil and always a story'. The story of Dolce & Gabbana itself though was only really just beginning.

'WE WORK IN FASHION,
BUT WE WORK FOR WOMEN.'

DOMENICO DOLCE

DONNA, DONNA

For Dolce and Gabbana, their mission is to decode and celebrate the essence of femininity as they see it. There are a number of women who, independently, have contributed to the very genetics of the Dolce & Gabbana brand. Inspired by them, the woman appearing on the Dolce & Gabbana catwalk has also grown more complex and sophisticated over the decades. American *Vogue*'s Vicki Woods concluded in 2009, 'Their women look fragile and feminine but utterly in control; powerful but romantic. Womanly.'

Of course the first and most important women to inspire Dolce and Gabbana were their mothers. Signora Gabbana, often to be found shrouded in an enormous fur and ready with a reprimand to smarten-up her son's look for the finale bow, provided the young Stefano with a primary icon. 'She is just very interested', Gabbana told *Vogue* in 2011. 'She is not in the business – she was a cleaner – but she loves fashion … she gave me the DNA.'

In an organza-lined fake-fur wrap coat of graduated strokes of grey from the autumn/winter 1992 collection titled simply The Trip, *supermodel Karen Mulder shows Dolce & Gabbana at their tactile best in an editorial for* Vogue *shot by Mikael Jansson.*

Domenico Dolce has talked of his mother's unflinching support when, aged 21, he told her about his homosexuality, and when he returned to Polizzi Generosa that despondent Christmas in 1985 it was she who proved instrumental in planning the adaptation of Dolce Saverio – the family tailoring business – to the manufacturing of her son and his partner's womenswear. In 2011, Dolce told *Vogue*: 'My family work in fashion – my father was a tailor and my mother had a clothes shop in Sicily. Even when we made crazy things she encouraged us, or if we had trouble she said she would always want to sort it out. The first show she applauded so much her palms were red raw.' The closeness of both designers to their mothers may well explain their celebratory approach to womanhood, one that does not force a woman to fit their vision but one that aims to develop and enhance her own attributes, reflecting her own vital personality. As Dolce said to *Vogue* in 2011, 'We work in fashion, but we work for women.'

After their mothers, their most identifiable icons are all performers, with cinema and music the source for the majority of Dolce & Gabbana's cast of muses. One of the pair's earliest-cited inspirations is the star of Italian Neorealist cinema Anna Magnani. 'One of the greatest Italian actresses, she was also a woman who dictated a very specific style,' wrote Franca Sozzani, the late editor-in-chief of *Vogue Italia*, explaining Magnani's influence on Dolce and Gabbana. The actress perfected the fiery, passionate and often tragic working-class heroine for directors such as Roberto Rossellini, Federico Fellini, Luchino Visconti and Pier Paolo Pasolini, and the designers borrowed both her wardrobe and her styling: a little black bag, an oversize overcoat or a sensual twinset or a shirt unbuttoned to mid-cleavage revealing flashes of a black bra. It is her personality that Dolce & Gabbana find most captivating, however, and have themselves captured it with remarkable success: if Magnani's brooding heart and wild emotion can be seen in a Dolce-&-Gabbana-dressed image, for them it will have done the garment justice.

The next great archetype of Italian womanhood that the designers fixated upon was Angelica Sedara in Lampedusa's grand epic *The Leopard*, more specifically Claudia Cardinale's Angelica who so utterly intoxicates Alain Delon's Tancredi in Luchino Visconti's 1963 film adaptation. Beginning with the *Il Gattopardo* collection in 1988, Dolce & Gabbana have frequently revisited not only Angelica's full skirts and bejewelled chignons but also her Italian temperament – at once dramatic, romantic and utterly seductive – and her setting of fragile yet exuberant baroque grandeur.

Jodie Kidd, photographed by Pamela Hanson on the streets of Paris for a December 1995 Vogue story entitled 'Capital Style'; her suit embodies the designers' introduction of a new cosmopolitan spirit to their classic Dolce Vita style, with a tomato-red hound's-tooth bouclé tweed jacket and matching skirt.

Overleaf *In Sicilian black lace and rose-print alpaca, models Karlie Kloss and Karmen Pedaru showcase twin sheaths of perfect proportion in a masterclass of cut, colour and craftsmanship, photographed by Daniel Jackson in 2010.*

'When we design it's like a movie. We think of a story and we design the clothes to go with it.'

DOLCE & GABBANA

'SICILIAN STYLE
FOR ME IS ABOUT A
PASSION FOR LIFE.
IT'S ABOUT ONE
COLOUR — BLACK
— THAT THEN
ABSORBS ALL THE
OTHER STRONGER
COLOURS.'

STEFANO GABBANA

As Dolce & Gabbana's suggestive but still chaste unbuttoned-ness morphed into a more potent expression of sexuality, they turned for inspiration to Sophia Loren. Across the entire span of their career, the almond-eyed and buxom Loren is the woman cited most often by Dolce & Gabbana as a muse. Perhaps what first seduced them was the black satin corset she wore to bamboozle Peter Sellers in *The Millionairess* in 1960; indeed it is a garment that has remained a key part of the Dolce & Gabbana armoury from almost the very beginning. It may also be the fact that Loren brings with her an inescapable, very southern Italian warmth and zext for life that is another key part of the brand's appeal. Like their other living muses, Loren has gone from distant fascination to become part of the Dolce & Gabbana family. Honoured in 2015 with her own shade of red Dolce & Gabbana lipstick (Sophia Loren No. 1, no less) the pair also cast Loren as their matriarch for an Ennio-Morricone-soundtracked television advert for the 2016 launch of their Dolce Rosa Excelsa perfume. Most recently, Dolce & Gabbana dedicated a sensational fashion show to Loren staged on the streets of her home town of Naples, with Loren guest of honour on her own throne as marching bands cheered the Neapolitan anthem 'Funiculì, Funiculà'.

An original house muse and bridge between Cinecittà-era cinema and new Hollywood, Isabella Rossellini is embraced by Dolce & Gabbana's marabou stole and photographed by Sante d'Orazio in 1991.

Whilst Dolce & Gabbana set about defining a canon of muses around which to build their imagined Italianate universe, they rapidly caught the eye of contemporary young women who shared a similar aesthetic urge. One of the first of these was actress Isabella Rossellini – daughter of Ingrid Bergman and of Roberto Rossellini, the director who worked particularly closely with Anna Magnani – who was introduced to the pair by *Vogue* photographer Steven Meisel in 1987. In a book published by the designers to mark their ten-year anniversary, Rossellini said: 'The first piece I wore from their collection was a white shirt, very chaste with a beautiful handmade embroidered collar. But the shirt was purposefully cut to make my breasts look as if they would burst out of it. It was Domenico and Stefano underlining and revealing a very Italian way of seduction. The unspoken, inexplicit

message of the woman that states, "No matter how much we try our bodies are so voluptuous that they cannot be contained in any clothes".' Dolce later recalled: 'Of course, Isabella understood Neorealism better than anyone: her father, Roberto Rossellini, invented it. She knew everything about being Italian. She even knows the village in Sicily I was born in.'

Rossellini took to the Dolce & Gabbana catwalk for a number of their early shows; she brought a theatrical quality that particularly enhanced the more androgynous elements of the feminised masculine tailoring for which Dolce & Gabbana were growing famous. Gabbana observed, 'There are many women inside of Isabella. The mother, the erotic type, the lover, the bad girl ...' This was seen to optimum effect in *Vogue*'s December 1991 issue where Rossellini appeared in a shot by Sante d'Orazio laid back in bliss wrapped only in white marabou and a lick of red lipstick. Rossellini, through lineage and her own attributes, can be seen to capture the mission of Dolce & Gabbana to present a modern femininity in fashion through interpretations of both contemporary and historical Italian-ness.

Supermodel Tatjana Patitz as a modern-day Venus in Dolce & Gabbana's ultra-glamorous cotton and lycra body encrusted with rows of radiant rhinestones. Photographed by Herb Ritts for Vogue's *'Modern Metallics' story in 1991.*

Dolce & Gabbana's original classical Italian feminine archetype evolved into something evoking a more international sense of glamour through collections such as the clingy, crystal-laden *Little Italy* collection for autumn/winter 1990. The star of that collection's seething and dramatic advertising campaign was Dolce & Gabbana's latest prima donna, Linda Evangelista, the Canadian supermodel born of Italian emigré parents. In the advertising campaign, Evangelista took on a range of roles, from brassy to browbeaten, returning alongside fellow supermodel Christy Turlington for the following season's campaign. In this, Gabbana asserted, 'Linda *became* Sophia Loren; her lips a little down at the corner, the cat eyes. Totally the same.'

With their spring/summer 1992 collection (called simply *La Dolce Vita*), Dolce & Gabbana's quintessential Italian heroine came to the attention of a growing international audience. Partly this was thanks to Linda Evangelista, who was so taken by the collection while being fitted that she telephoned a roster of her fellow supermodels – including Naomi Campbell, Cindy Crawford, Yasmeen Ghauri, Tatjana Patitz, Carla Bruni and Helena Christensen – who all agreed to model the collection in exchange for clothes (Gabbana later said that they all wanted corsets). The collection, perhaps the pair's most provocative yet, was all-out glamour, figuratively (and occasionally literally) spelling out *SEX* in rhinestone and with suspended stockings, marabou trim and cinched corsetry. *Women's Wear Daily* described it as 'an ode to Barbarella and Frederick's of Hollywood' [the sexy science-fiction film and the lingerie specialists]. Rossellini also returned to the runway, alongside another long-term Dolce & Gabbana model and friend Monica Bellucci, herself a successful actress of growing repute at home in Italy and abroad. A masterclass in boudoir dressing appropriated for the street, *La Dolce Vita* particularly appealed to a new friend of the house, one who represented the perfect embodiment of Dolce & Gabbana's projection of Italian femininity onto a modern and international stage.

Alla Kostromicheva, photographed by Daniel Jackson, brings a harder, more modern edge to a classic feminine silhouette wearing Dolce & Gabbana's black lace skirt and signature corset, its base structured like the top of a crinoline – 'a confection of tulle and lace' said Vogue in 2010.

The designers had first met Madonna in late 1989 when she was filming *Dick Tracy* in New York. They had excitedly spotted her wearing a black crochet design of theirs in a party picture in the *International Herald Tribune* and contacted her to offer more pieces. A dinner in Chelsea led to a night of clubbing and an after party chez Madonna, and an enduring friendship began. For the 1991 New York premiere of her documentary *In Bed With Madonna* (*Truth or Dare* in the US) – in which she declared his gift of a Dolce & Gabbana shirt as Warren Beatty's route to her heart – La Ciccone donned a top-to-toe look of jewel-encrusted body and black stockings that confirmed her deep affinity with the Dolce & Gabbana brand of sexy subversion.

Madonna shared many of Dolce & Gabbana's preoccupations: sex, provocation, using religious iconography in a creative but nevertheless sacrilegious way, and her Italian heritage. She also was – and of course remains – one of the world's pre-eminent and most

recognisable stars. Celebrity and the fashion industry were becoming closely entwined, something that Dolce and Gabbana were increasingly intrigued by. Most specifically, she was demonstrating how one could grow an international following whilst keeping a sense of subversion. With the house becoming more firmly ensconced within the Milan fashion establishment and now selling in 350 stores around the world, Madonna as high priestess of controversy appealed to a duo wishing to retain their edge.

Their involvement with Madonna led to a controversy within the Italian fashion establishment when Dolce & Gabbana held a dinner in Madonna's honour at the same time as Giorgio Armani's Emporio show at the Milan spring/summer 1993 collections in October 1992, thus challenging the loyalties of the fashion press. Responding to accusations that the designers had paid Madonna $500,000 to appear in an effort to sabotage their rival, Gabbana vowed to *The New York Times*, 'I would swear in front of the real Madonna we did not pay'.

At the 1991 New York premiere for her film In Bed With Madonna *(Truth or Dare), the star looked sensational in a Dolce & Gabbana corset covered in multicoloured stones and charms from autumn/winter 1991's* Le Pin Up *collection.*

Madonna had certainly been seduced by Dolce & Gabbana and would go on to wear a number of custom-made pieces for her Girlie Show world tour the following year. Of the house's appeal she said, 'Now that Fellini, Rossellini, Pasolini and Visconti are gone, all we have is Dolce & Gabbana: neo-realistic fashion.' More recently Madonna appeared as a dishwashing, spaghetti-devouring matriarch in black-and-white scenes of neo-Neorealism for the spring/summer 2010 advertising campaign.

Whilst women came first for Dolce & Gabbana, men were not too far behind. Launching their menswear line in 1989, the pair told Italian *L'Uomo Vogue* they were fixated on dressing 'a modern man, without prejudice and attached to traditional values', citing both the aristocratic airs of Visconti's leading men and the 'rags' of traditional Sicilian workmen. Their early menswear carried with it the sensuality of their womenswear and focused particularly on knitwear. For the time being Dolce & Gabbana would leave cashmere to the older masters, favouring coarse, thick and loosely woven wools in raw and earthy shades to reflect their rustic and rugged archetype.

Alongside their woman, the Dolce & Gabbana man has his own distinct personality, if somewhat less informed by specific real-life and fictional icons. The Dolce & Gabbana man's closest living relative is the working Sicilian at leisure, who over the years has frequently returned to the catwalk in ribbed white vest, draped in his fishing nets, or donning an urchin-like *coppola* flat cap. For spring/summer 2013 this Sicilian became truly incarnate on the catwalk, as Domenico and Stefano cast a number of men and boys from villages and towns across Sicily to embody their tale of Sicilian folklore and the Ages of Man. This approach lasted for a number of seasons and is frequently incorporated into the casting of their menswear shows.

The culture of competitive sport is a leading influence on the look of the Dolce & Gabbana man, reflected here in a Vogue Men shoot by Peggy Sirota of a ribbed wool sweater and cotton jersey shorts from the spring/ summer 1991 collection.

Other men that naturally inhabit the Dolce & Gabbana world are those the designers see as modern-day gladiators: sportsmen. From the publication of *Calcio (Soccer)* in 2003, a Mariano Vivanco-shot tome of footballers in Dolce & Gabbana, the brand has retained strong links with the sporting world. Both AC Milan and Chelsea FC have been dressed in suits by Dolce & Gabbana for appearances off the pitch, and members of Italian national teams from cycling to swimming and, of course, football have stripped down for various underwear advertising campaigns.

If one figure has to come to embody the Dolce & Gabbana man in recent years, it is the sportsmanlike physique of David Gandy, who emerged from relative obscurity in 2006 to star in Dolce & Gabbana's Light Blue fragrance campaign shot by Mario Testino. Here, in a pair of white swimming trunks enjoying a secluded lagoon and a dinghy with a comparatively covered-up Marija Vujovic, Gandy and the campaign launched a wave of passionate, almost hysterical admiration and a hugely successful global modelling career. For all its camp, it is worth highlighting that the Light Blue campaign emerged during a period of men's fashion where the sole male ideal was that of a pale, teenage ectomorphic waif. Through Gandy and his

sporting compatriots, Dolce & Gabbana have helped to reintroduce the hyper-athletic to the forefront of fashion.

Having introduced ideal men and women, inevitably Dolce & Gabbana now provide for an entire family, with that quintessentially Italian multi-generational affection reflected in everything from Dolce & Gabbana's childrenswear, launched in 2012 to recent campaigns featuring selfie-taking, garlanded and gossiping grandmothers. For a label so proudly Italian, it makes sense for Dolce & Gabbana to build a business around *la famiglia*, even coining the Instagram tag #DGFamily as part of their social media presence, celebrating the broad (if almost exclusively gorgeous) range of groups and individuals welcomed into their fold.

Sporting the white bathing trunks immortalised in the Light Blue fragrance campaign that he has fronted – with a succession of female co-stars – for over a decade, David Gandy takes to the catwalk at Dolce & Gabbana's spring/ summer 2007 menswear show in Milan.

Their reverence for the traditional structure of the Italian family brought controversy for the designers in 2015 following a collection entitled *Viva la Mamma*, dedicated to mothers and featuring several children on the catwalk too. In an interview for the Italian news magazine *Panorama*, Dolce said: 'You are born and you have a father and a mother. At least it should be like that.' This and further comments by Dolce about non-traditional methods of conception acted – once translated into English – as the spark for a fast-burning social media firestorm. Soon afterwards the designers moved to clarify their position, and apologised for causing offence. In an interview with *Details* magazine Gabbana emphasised he had told the same interviewer of his own desire to have children. Dolce added: 'The writer asked me to talk about the concept of family. So I talked about what I have grown up with, my culture, the Italian idea of family. Whether you are gay, not gay, whether you have a baby or not, whatever you do – it is your choice and it is no business of mine … I am just a tailor, and I talk with the words I have.'

Today, the members of the Dolce & Gabbana family featuring on its billboards are of all ages, countries and kinds, reflecting the multi-faceted consumer base it now has as a major, multi-billion-dollar international brand. Its roots, however, are always traceable back to Mother Italy.

'ITALIANS KNOW THAT WHAT MATTERS IS STYLE, NOT FASHION.'

STEFANO GABBANA

Proving Dolce & Gabbana's transformative power, Russian-born American singer-songwriter Regina Spektor becomes a voluptuous Mediterranean femme fatale in a black silk-satin corset dress. Photographed by Nick Knight in 2007.

'I HOPE THE PEOPLE REMEMBER
DOLCE & GABBANA FOR
THE SENSUALITY, FOR THE
MEDITERRANEAN SENSE, FOR
OUR HONESTY TO THE LIFE.'

DOMENICO DOLCE

CATHOLIC TASTES

The 1990s having begun for Dolce & Gabbana as an exercise in defining their international but ultimately Italian woman, the pair soon began to take on a less geographically limited approach, reflecting their experiences of visiting new, once exotic locations as their brand grew around the world. Entitled *The Trip*, the autumn/winter 1992 collection was a modern-day Grand Tour. Showing an even more confident sexuality, with visible suspender straps, black corsets and roses nestled amongst cleavage, these designs were shown against more dandy-like ones of patchworked-velvet suits and silks in prints of collaged city names. The result was both eclectic and assured, with *New York* magazine concluding that 'more and more, the bright flashes that were hidden in their collections have come to dominate the foreground'. Dolce himself explained: 'This woman has shown she is beautiful. Now she wants to show her mind.'

From here the journey continued, with much of the Nineties finding Dolce & Gabbana exploring disparate starting points in time and space to take their increasingly sophisticated woman. Examining a list of the names given to the collections shows this variety, taking us everywhere from *The Seventies* for spring/summer 1993 (the perfect excuse to further explore the louche velvets that were now decidedly a house signature), to *The OrientExpress* the following season. This collection inspired *Vogue* to take its own travels, resulting in a soft and sensual portrait of Kate Moss in claret empire-line chiffon on the streets of Kathmandu.

These sojourns had allowed Dolce & Gabbana to explore not just new themes but new techniques and fabrics, expanding their repertoire. They were, however, aware of the business-led need to base this exploration around house 'codes' in a manner comfortingly recognisable for buyers yet novel enough to tempt wallets from pockets. They soon reminded themselves that at the heart of Dolce & Gabbana is an essential Italianness, and a quality perhaps more particular to Sicily.

The deceptively simple, classic lines of Dolce & Gabbana's richly coloured soft chiffon dress photographed by Arthur Elgort in Nepal in 1993.

Overleaf *A sultry Cindy Crawford stalks the runway in black lingerie lace – complete with freshly cut rose – for Dolce & Gabbana's autumn/winter 1992 The Trip collection.*

'THEY EMPHASISE PARTS OF THE FEMALE ANATOMY — BREASTS AND HIPS — THAT OTHER, MORE TAILORING-MINDED ITALIAN DESIGNERS OFTEN PRETEND DON'T EXIST.'

VOGUE

'DESIGNERS WHO COMBINE THE NAUGHTINESS OF THE BOUDOIR WITH THE BAROQUE FORMALITY OF THE SICILIAN ARISTOCRACY.'

THE NEW YORKER

From Vogue's 'Glamour is Back' issue in November 1993, Nick Knight shoots Linda Evangelista in Dolce & Gabbana's black satin-backed crêpe dress with 'vermicelli' straps, under a patchworked chiffon and lace shirt with ruffle front.

So, returning somewhat closer to home for spring 1994, they looked to what Gabbana described as 'parts of the Mediterranean we consider hidden treasures' for a collection that drew on the theatrical (contrasting the operatic volumes of Maria Callas' stage costumes with refined, androgynous silhouettes based on 'The Tramp'-era Charlie Chaplin), with exotic fabrics and embellishments drawn from the extremities of the Mediterranean, from Northern Africa to the Near East. Soft black veils indicated 'an innocence' the pair cited as reflecting a softer, less aggressive sexuality, as well as a way to 'still use transparent fabrics without revealing too much skin'. Called *Mediterraneo*, the collection also explored the myriad cultural influences that have influenced the label's spiritual home of Sicily over centuries of international invasion, thus allowing them to reconcile a wide selection of themes yet remain true to the character of the label.

As well as finding new inspirations, Dolce & Gabbana explored experimental fabric combinations, displayed by Amber Valletta to startling effect in a herringbone tweed and PVC double-breasted jacket with fake-fur collar and cuffs, photographed by Mario Testino in 1994.

Another central pillar of Dolce & Gabbana is the mastery of feminine tailoring. This was explored through 113 different fabrics in the *New Rock 'n' Roll* collection for autumn/winter 1994, a remarkable expression of their skill in interpreting the traditions of men's suiting for the modern woman. Snippy short skirt suits in tough worsted and full-length black sheaths with short trains paired with flat brogues displayed a masculine-feminine quality. The contrast of tradition and forward-thinking was encapsulated in tweed overlaid with transparent PVC, a 'projection into the future' interpreted with complete confidence for *Vogue* by Mario Testino in a shot of Amber Valletta, tidying her brow at the bathroom mirror, in a herringbone jacket with the lower half replaced with the see-through plastic, showing both her and Dolce & Gabbana's own perfectly-pitched cheek.

Cinema had first enraptured the designers with singular heroines, but by the mid-Nineties Dolce & Gabbana took a look at the medium with new breadth and depth, incorporating a cinematic quality into the brand at all levels, from the presentation of catwalk collections to its advertising campaigns. As modern starlets flocked to wear the label

on the red carpet and at work and play, Dolce & Gabbana looked back to Hollywood's Golden Age with the spring/summer 1995 *Hollywood Glamour* collection. Drawing on the powerfully seductive adoption of the man's smoking jacket and silk pyjama, as done by early twentieth-century starlets and another Dolce & Gabbana style heroine, Coco Chanel, the cinematic tone was enhanced by the return of Isabella Rossellini to the catwalk, whom the pair described backstage as 'the symbol of an Italian woman who lives outside of Italy'. Rossellini was joined by actress Monica Bellucci, continuing the film-star theme, who had been modelling for the label since 1989 and had starred in their self-titled debut fragrance campaign in 1995. For *Vogue*, the story was captured in a Raymond Meier close-up of Yasmeen Ghauri nestled in glittery blue Busby Berkeley-style crescent moon. Contemporary Hollywood was brought in via Drew Barrymore's appearance in the magazine as a modern-day Mae West in Dolce & Gabbana's lingerie lace. Dolce & Gabbana remained on a cinematic note for autumn/winter 1995 where they based a collection on Luis Buñuel's seminal film *Belle de Jour*, a reference that allowed them to mix cinema, sex and subversion in an immensely saleable selection of neat wool skirt suits, A-line dresses and coats. By March 1995 Dolce & Gabbana had dressed their first Oscar-winner, placing Susan Sarandon in mocha-hued full-skirted satin to collect her Best Actress award for *Dead Man Walking*.

However subversive their inspiration, Dolce & Gabbana's superbly tailored neat skirt suits were perfect for the working woman's wardrobe. In strawberry-milkshake-shaded crêpe, model Yasmeen Ghauri is at once arch and innocent in pin-sharp pencil skirt and matching jacket, photographed by Neil Kirk in 1995.

Overleaf *In a feather shrug and diamanté-peppered pink crêpe from the spring/summer 1995* Hollywood Glamour *collection Ghauri returns nestled in the crescent of a shiny blue moon. Photograph by Raymond Meier.*

For many, the perfect marriage of Italy and cinema lies in the work of Federico Fellini, and his wit and subversion make him a perfect inspiration for Dolce & Gabbana. His heroines had appeared in collections from the start, but his films were now directly referenced, first in autumn/winter 1996's *Le Notti di Cabiria*-inspired collection. As Domenico Dolce explained, the ideas originated from a single still, of a woman in a herringbone coat getting into a car. 'All you see is her back, and a flash of black-seamed stockings as she climbs in.'

'POWERFUL BUT ROMANTIC. WOMANLY.'

VOGUE

Around this erotic severity came stiff car coats, buttoned pencil skirts, carved tailoring and corsetry, with the camper whimsy of Cabiria herself (a Roman prostitute looking hopelessly for love) served in frothy, yet elegant and feminine floral chiffons whipped into gossamer-light sheaths over corsetry.

D olce & Gabbana revisited Fellini for autumn/winter 1997, this time citing his 1972 epic, *Roma*. This collection drew on the film's ecclesiastical costuming, creating strict and sensual full-length buttoned cassock coats and tops emblazoned with icons of the Madonna and child. This union of cinema and Roman Catholicism has provided Dolce & Gabbana with one of its most enduring themes, threading through the decades, perhaps most inventively in the spring/summer 2013 Hitchcock-meets-Byzantine collection where curvacious peplums paired with prints lifted from the mosaicked walls of the Cattedrale di Santa Maria Nuova in the Sicilian town of Monreale.

The purity of a white stretch-silk chiffon dress with geometric seams and boning, from autumn/winter 1997's Roma-inspired collection, looks perfect on the clean and classic beauty of Kirsty Hume. Photograph by Tom Munro.

Overleaf *Religious imagery and themes return time and again for Dolce & Gabbana. With the kitsch charm of a Vatican souvenir, a portable sequin-strewn shrine of a handbag (left) is photographed by Raymond Meier in 1998. Carolyn Murphy models a glittery Madonna and child top and embroidered headscarf (right) for spring/ summer 1998's Stromboli collection. Photograph by Andrew Lamb.*

The very fabrics of church – brocade, crimson velvet, white lace, black veiling and that very Catholic gilt – pervade the atmosphere of every show almost like incense. It is what gives their underlying (or, often, overwritten) sexuality such a wicked frisson. Whilst the traditions, rites and rituals of Catholicism appeal profoundly to the Dolce & Gabbana sensibility, they are necessarily balanced with a more modern attitude that appears often through innovation in craftsmanship.

Inspired by a summer holiday in Stromboli, for spring/summer 1998 Dolce & Gabbana recreated everything from the headscarves of its working women (this time elevated with intricate floral embroidery) to its summertime butterflies settling in kaleidoscopic patterns on a number of swagged-tulle bodices with breezy bias-cut skirts. However, the soft, nostalgic mood was countered by a number of acid-bright latex dresses, which *Vogue* praised as Dolce & Gabbana 'taking the dress into the twenty-first century'.

In using tradition to inspire invention Dolce & Gabbana often pay tribute to those fellow fashion designers past and present whom they admire. Even the leopard print, which is such a recognisable part of the house's handwriting, they acknowledge is a tribute to Yves St Laurent, a designer they frequently reference in admiration of his virtuosity in cut and colour. For autumn/winter 1998, Dolce & Gabbana honoured two mid-century masters of haute couture, Christian Dior and Cristóbal Balenciaga, in a collection focused on the two key aspects of the medium: *tailleur* (tailoring) and *flou* (soft dressmaking). The collection incorporated a sense of fashion futurism enhanced by a series of mercurial silver lamé dresses built on a foundation of intricately boned corsetry.

The designers continued to explore futuristic themes. With their spring/summer 1999 collection, wryly named *The New Black*, the duo looked at the new working woman's wardrobe, based around the classic little black dress. Many designs came accessorised with a utilitarian, new-century take on the maid's apron, set askew: a nod to how far the notion of woman's work had come. The collection also came with a new high-tech holographic fabric, developed by Dolce & Gabbana, carved into body-conscious shifts and pencil skirts. This stride toward a brave new world was interpreted by Nathaniel Goldberg for *Vogue* on model Amber Valletta in a Dolce & Gabbana iridescent sheath, marching down a staircase that looked like the set from Fritz Lang's science-fiction film *Metropolis*. By autumn/winter 1999, a huge variety of materials, including goat hair, tartan, denim and tie-dyed fur, were added to the leopard print, plastic and holographic PVC that were already part of the house's eclectic elements. Christened *Kitsch*, this collection fully distinguished itself from the decade's prevailing minimalism, with Gabbana later telling American *Vogue*, 'I don't know if we have good taste or bad taste – but we have a taste!'

At the close of the millennium, Dolce & Gabbana embarked on a series of experiments with fabric to invigorate the classic shapes they had established as perfect for womankind in any era. Here, Amber Valletta models a cleanly cut strapless sheath in shimmering blue laser hologram vinyl photographed by Nathaniel Goldberg in 1999.

'ITALY HAS THE
BEST QUALITIES
AND YOU WAKE
UP TO A CULTURE
OF BEAUTY.'

DOMENICO DOLCE

Dolce & Gabbana's signature
leopard print is an enduring
motif. Photographed by Tom
Craig, model Angela Lindvall
has the air of a glamorous
runaway in a scarlet silk
leopard-print dress from the
spring/summer 2010 Sicilian
Sensuality collection.

Overleaf Crystal
embellishment is another
enduring Dolce & Gabbana
theme. In a 2004 Vogue
story entitled 'Deadlier than
the Male' Paolo Roversi
photographs Elise Crombez
oozing film-noir drama in a
chiffon bias-cut gown traced
with crystal.

'TWO DIFFERENT
PATHS, A COMMON
VISION OF FASHION,
THE SAME IDEA
OF "WOMAN".'

VOGUE ITALIA

The eclectic theme continued through to the following spring's *Mix and Match* collection, shown amongst a set made up as a traditional Sicilian market stall, complete with heckling barrow boys. It was another cornucopia of print and fabrics, with leopard-print hosiery and bikinis exposed through open shirts keeping the thread of continuity. As 'bling' seeped out of hip hop culture and into the mainstream, Dolce & Gabbana reflected this with a crystal mesh fabric used at times to hem cropped tops and hipster trousers in 10cm/4in wide bands, and others in entire jackets and coats.

At the turn of the millennium, Dolce & Gabbana was now a vast fashion empire with annual sales comfortably above $300 million. This had afforded them a lavish lifestyle with residences in Roquebrune-Cap-Martin on the French Riviera (later sold), the island of Stromboli off the Sicilian coast and a lavish property (originally three separate apartments) in Milan. The duplex, created to the designers' exacting tastes in collaboration with the architects Claudio Nardi and Rodolfo Dordoni had a rooftop garden and was the subject of a Hamish Bowles profile in the May 2000 issue of American *Vogue*. A perfect reflection of the Dolce & Gabbana style, with leopard-print rife on wallpaper and upholstery throughout, the house reflected the increasingly opulent extravagance of their fashion designs. Explaining the link, Gabbana told Bowles that 'our job is our life, our life our job'.

Nick Knight photographs a sleek and sexy Claudia Schiffer wearing a collision of prints from the Kitsch collection of autumn/winter 1999 for a portfolio honouring Vogue's greatest models.

Overleaf *The autumn/winter 2000 collection was inspired by artist Tamara de Lempicka and in this appropriately Art-Deco styled image by John Akehurst, a pleated silk-chiffon dress is worn over a pair of oriental cropped brocade trousers and gold sandals.*

The designers also developed a careful aesthetic for their retail spaces. These sumptuous emporia, with changing rooms built for couples to try on and compare outfits together, reflect *Gattopardo* levels of luxe, with gilt mirrors, marble and deep patterned carpets. In turn, the decoration of their own home has provided inspiration for collections, most notably for autumn/winter 2000, where a 1926 Tamara de Lempicka portrait – a Christmas gift from Stefano to Domenico hanging in their Milan mansion – provoked an expression of languorous Art Deco laid against wallpaper-flocked brocades.

Though the first decade of the new millennium perhaps saw the designers exploring the Italian personality of the brand less consistently, their designs would retain enough of the core identity with tailoring, corsetry, artisanal embroideries and sumptuous fabrics. Dolce & Gabbana's heroines were one vehicle for maintaining continuity, and for spring/summer 2001 they joined forces with an old friend. In early 2000 Madonna asked for something cowboy-like to wear in her video for 'Don't Tell Me'. Dolce recalled that 'her ideas were completely in sync with bits of the collection we were already working on: the jewelled leather and suede fringed pants that were in the show and the jeans that had satin inserts that made them look like chaps'. Their spring/summer 2001 runway collection was dedicated to and named for Madonna; into a display of slick and sharp crystal-embellished tailoring and Western-style denim, the designers incorporated several tributes to the singer in the form of 'greatest hits' t-shirts emblazoned with record cover images.

By the time of the spring/summer 2002 *Latina* collection they had their own South American heroine: Brazilian bombshell (and the world's highest-paid model) Gisele Bündchen had become the house favourite, starring in most of their advertising campaigns and opening the majority of their womenswear shows. In 2003, Dolce and Gabbana brought her to the *Vogue*-chaired gala to celebrate the opening of the *Goddess* exhibition at the Metropolitan Museum in New York, along with a new member of their own circle (and now fashion icon in her own right) Victoria Beckham.

Gisele Bündchen's Brazilian roots and German heritage perfectly captured Dolce & Gabbana's world-spanning inspirations. Here she wears a paisley silk-chiffon dress from the spring/ summer 2002 Latina *collection Photograph by Thomas Schenk.*

Overleaf *Photographed by Nick Knight, Victoria Beckham wears a tulle and organdie dress from spring/ summer 2008.*

'Unabashed exuberance, with tongue
placed firmly in cheek.'

TIM BLANKS, VOGUE.COM

'THEIR WOMEN LOOK FRAGILE AND FEMININE BUT UTTERLY IN CONTROL.'

VOGUE

Inspired by the exhibition, the designers conceived a collection of goddess-worthy dresses to present for the finale of their autumn/winter 2003 *Techno Romantic* collection, culminating in a breathtaking creation of bias-cut, crystal-embellished transparent grey chiffon, a perfect paradigm for Dolce & Gabbana's confident eroticism and classical romance. The finale dress reappeared in a photograph by Mario Testino for *Vogue*'s December issue, with model Elise Crombez posed poetically, as if an Aphrodite of some ancient frieze.

The love for Dolce's birthplace was reiterated with the launch of the perfume Sicily in late 2003. Monica Bellucci returned as its promotional star, described by Gabbana as 'passionate, dramatic, quintessentially Italian'. The campaign reinforced the Italian soul of the company while the mainline collections continued to explore diverse inspirations. The spring/summer 2004 collection was a case in point, a time-travelling show that featured myriad historical silhouettes from Twenties flappers, Sixties go-go girls and Thirties screen sirens all the way up to a thoroughly modern sex symbol in a gravity-defying cutout swimsuit. Flowing through the collection and uniting it was a breeze of psychedelic chiffon designs described by *Vogue*'s Hamish Bowles as a 'print-on-print delirium', shown off to great effect by model Daria Werbowy in a multi-tiered flirty flower-girl look photographed by Tesh for *Vogue*.

Elise Crombez becomes a heroine of romance for Vogue's 'When Midnight Strikes' story photographed by Mario Testino in a handmade silk-chiffon fishtail gown from autumn/winter 2003 with darts of lace and an overlaid chainmail of Swarovski crystal.

***Overleaf** Swarovski crystals appeared again in Dolce & Gabbana's spring/summer 2004 collection, in a glittering striped flapper dress, captured in motion for Vogue by Richard Bush.*

'A dreamlike Sicily, far away, full of symbols and suggestion, which are hidden and not given.'

DOMENICO DOLCE

For autumn/winter 2004 the pair paid tribute to legendary photographer Helmut Newton, who had died just weeks before the show. Dolce & Gabbana had first worked with Newton for their first men's fragrance campaign and Gabbana described an evident affinity with Newton's 'unique world of sleek, sexy, powerful women'. For these women, Dolce & Gabbana went back to their greatest hits, making them sharp and seductive, from the humble grey cardigan (buttoned just so) to the more overt leopard print and reworked masculine tailoring, which paid perfect homage to Newton's iconic image of Yves Saint Laurent's Le Smoking tuxedo. A second and definitive paean to Saint Laurent and the photographers who helped make icons of his work began with a safari Dolce and Gabbana had taken and then had thought about in relation to Saint Laurent's definitive 1967 *Safari* collection. The moodboard for the spring 2005 *Africa* collection was strewn with *Vogue* images: 'Avedon for the beauty, and Penn for Africa', according to Gabbana, who had poignantly received news of Avedon's death as the collection – in sheets of snakeskin spliced with lingerie lace – was beginning to take shape.

D olce & Gabbana – and Domenico and Stefano – had travelled far from their origins to the status of superstars in command of a billion-dollar brand, and their original embattled Magnani-like muse had become a bona fide *La Dolce Vita* diva. Although their inspirations ranged widely, as fashion critic Tim Blanks explained: 'What unifies and makes such a success of all these disparate statements [is] unabashed exuberance, with tongue placed firmly in cheek'. By the middle of the 2000s, the designers themselves had enjoyed a remarkably successful personal and professional partnership lasting longer than the average marriage. As they approached the twentieth anniversary of their house, they were to prove that there would be further evolutions of Dolce & Gabbana the brand, and new passions for Dolce and Gabbana the men.

Daria Werbowy photographed by Tesh wearing a tiered dress of psychedelic silk-chiffon layers. The riot of colour continues with floral tights and hot pink wedge sandals, all taken from the aptly named Flower Power *collection of spring/ summer 2004.*

Overleaf *The joyful theatricality of Dolce & Gabbana's designs have made them a perfect fit for stars of the silver screen, on and off the red carpet. Sandra Bullock appears statuesque in leopard-print fishtail chiffon (left) photographed by Mario Testino in 1996. Sienna Miller dazzles in a tulle dress awash with crystal (right) for Nick Knight's December 2007* Vogue *cover.*

VOGUE

DEC
£3.70

SIENNA MILLER
Supergirl

60 PIECES FOR INSTANT PARTY WOW

The Glamour issue

WHO'S GLAMOROUS NOW

STAR QUALITY
Kate Moss and
Naomi Campbell
shine on

FASHION'S BIG NIGHT OUT

'I'M LUCKY BECAUSE I MET DOMENICO
IN MY LIFE — AND I THINK HE'S LUCKY
TO HAVE MET ME TOO.'

STEFANO GABBANA

A STRANGE ALCHEMY

In February 2005, an interview in the Italian newspaper *Corriere della Sera* revealed that Domenico Dolce and Stefano Gabbana were no longer involved in a romantic relationship. Asserting that Dolce & Gabbana was to continue with both at the creative helm, Dolce assured: 'On a professional level, we are still together. We work together wonderfully well, we have a very strong understanding. What happens in the past is still there, it continues and will continue forever.' In actual fact the couple had separated a few years before, with only family and a number of close friends made aware in a bid to protect both the pair's privacy and the image of the fashion house.

A mysterious scene of classic Vogue storytelling features model Rie Rasmussen as a modern Cinderella in Dolce & Gabbana's apple green chiffon and lace for photographer Norbert Schoerner on location in Russia in 2005.

Inevitably, for two designers so inextricably tied to their brand (and who had once quipped at being asked if they were equal partners, 'today, yes. One of us may get tired and then we'll sell the "&".'), intense speculation followed the output of subsequent collections, initially for signs of whether the label could survive the seemingly seismic shift. The news also brought renewed interest in the two very distinct roles the designers held as well as their two opposite but complementary personalities.

Dolce & Gabbana's corporate mission statement explains in its first chapter, 'the group's strength is based on the complementarity between the designers'. Stefano Gabbana told *Vogue* in 2010, 'really it is a strange alchemy. We were the first designer duo in 1984, and our relationship is strange, as we were lovers and we are not any more. It's more like family now, like brothers.' Though unlike brothers, for Dolce and Gabbana there is seemingly no sense of competition felt by either; each other's distinct strengths are encouraged and nurtured to powerful effect. Disagreement and discussion, however, form an essential part of the creative process. 'He has one taste, I have another. He tries to convince me and I try to convince him – we fight about silly things and very important things', Gabbana told *Vogue*, 'We have different perspectives. He's a tailor and gets upset about jackets, details, shoulder proportions. I'm more flamboyant, more instinctive.'

The choosing of fabrics often features early in Dolce & Gabbana's approach and is an aspect both designers participate in collectively and equally. The design process from there on is divided quite cleanly between the two, with Dolce the architect of the silhouette through tailoring and Gabbana involved in the more *flou*, softer, aspects of dressmaking, and the look and styling of an outfit as it comes together. 'Domenico is more Yves Saint Laurent, while I'm more Fiorucci', Gabbana explained to *The Guardian* in 2000, characterising himself as the modernising stylist to Dolce's more old-world couturier. As John Seabrook posited of Gabbana in a *New Yorker* profile of the pair in September 2005, 'he is the eyes for Dolce's hands'. Other areas require one designer to take greater responsibility over the other. The menswear for example, with its reliance on tailoring and reference to Sicilian workwear, is overseen predominantly by Dolce, whereas the youthful whimsicality of D&G arose more directly from the party-loving Gabbana, the self-confessed night owl of the two.

Where backstage at a fashion show and in interviews Dolce and Gabbana will largely speak as a united front, often finishing one another's sentences, Gabbana's more open and extroverted nature lends him more willingly to the vast public and media relations aspect expected of today's high-profile designers. His enjoyment has even led to a small number of acting and presenting roles in various productions for Italian television over the years. When top fashion editors come to view a collection just ahead of its presentation, it is quite likely that Gabbana will field questions whilst Dolce perfects the hem of a trouser or the slope of a shoulder. As for the business of running Dolce & Gabbana S.p.A, Gabbana confides that it is Dolce who takes a keener interest though Dolce vouches for Gabbana's innate ability to pick out a bestseller from any collection.

Model Malgosia Bela in Dolce & Gabbana's soft frills and glittery layers: a raspberry-coloured ruffled pencil skirt and pale pink silk blouse with matching collar from autumn/winter 2009's Surrealism *collection. Photograph by Josh Olins.*

Overleaf *Showcasing the finely tuned androgyny perfected through Dolce tailoring, Tim Gutt photographs model Siri Tollerød in 2010 posing as a matador, wearing a cropped wool jacket with satin shirt and cigarillo-slim wool trousers.*

'We look at the same things with two different points of view – but we arrive at the same place.'

DOMENICO DOLCE

'WE BUILT
OUR FASHION
AROUND THREE
FUNDAMENTAL
CONCEPTS:
SICILY, TAILORING,
AND TRADITION.'

DOMENICO DOLCE

By the end of their twentieth year in business, Dolce & Gabbana had joined the most exclusive club, that of the billion-dollar brands. Through co-operation and allowing each other personal freedom, they had not only made their partnership last beyond their romance, but had in fact made a success of what they have seen as their family – their house and all who worked there with them. To celebrate the twentieth anniversary of their first stand-alone show, an epic 98-look presentation for spring/summer 2006 took the essence of Dolce & Gabbana and magnified it. It was in four parts, from red to white, then black and culminating in a barnstorming finale of ballgowns in gingham check, cascading rose print and feathers, after which Dolce & Gabbana walked down the catwalk hand in hand, showing that they and their ampersand were here to stay. Even aside from the gingham that hinted at dresses worn by Brigitte Bardot, the collection could easily have been called after her film *And God Created Woman*, with the parade of models all sporting the bosom, bursting hips and irresistible wiggle so adored by Dolce & Gabbana since the early days. In tribute, *Vogue* put these ingredients into its May cover in one look, with Natalia Vodianova its beautifully buxom cover star.

For the following spring, the designers took this sexy, curvaceous look far into the future, dipping the exaggerated-bust-and-hip silhouette into chrome and stripping it back to its essence in transparent latex. Both looks were seized upon by *Vogue* in editorials that commended their harder, more sexual sensuality as a counterpoint to the rather demure and sedate landscape of the season.

Supermodel Natalia Vodianova is the classic image of feminine seduction in a broderie anglaise bodice with a frayed-fringe trim, photographed by Patrick Demarchelier in 2006.

Overleaf *Jessica Stam becomes Maria from Fritz Lang's pioneering science-fiction film* Metropolis *in a plastic corset dress, accessorised with a custom case for the newly released iPhone, as Dolce & Gabbana pushed their brand of super-sexy eveningwear into the future. Photographed by Liz Collins in 2007.*

'Our woman is *supersensuale* and *iperfemminile*.'

DOMENICO DOLCE

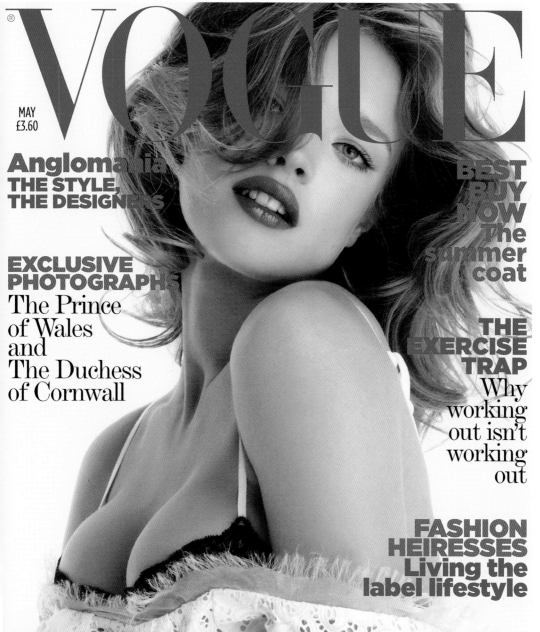

VOGUE

MAY
£3.60

Angloma fa
THE STYLE,
THE DESIGNERS

EXCLUSIVE
PHOTOGRAPHS
The Prince
of Wales
and
The Duchess
of Cornwall

BEST
BUY
NOW
The
summer
coat

THE
EXERCISE
TRAP
Why
working
out isn't
working
out

FASHION
HEIRESSES
Living the
label lifestyle

KISS ME QUICK

The colour of summer dressing

'A UNIQUE WORLD OF SLEEK, SEXY, POWERFUL WOMEN.'

STEFANO GABBANA

The Dolce & Gabbana curve reached its apex in autumn/winter 2007, where the designers sent out model after model in crystal-embellished evening gowns cinched in with a provocative metal 'chastity' belt, complete with padlock. This became the most wanted accessory of the awards season, and showed their nous in acknowledging that the red carpet was now a fully fledged extension of the catwalk. A somewhat less-expected piece of publicity, however, was the appearance of Naomi Campbell on her last day of a week-long community service stint in New York, clocking off for the last time in the full catwalk look with the little padlock swinging all the way to a waiting limousine.

Resplendent in Dolce & Gabbana, Naomi Campbell leaves the last of five days' community service at a Manhattan sanitation garage in March 2007. Heading from her final shift straight to Elton John's 60th birthday party, Campbell topped a week of commuting-cum-catwalking with this full-length Swarovski-encrusted gown, to the delight of the waiting paparazzi.

A very different sensibility, both cerebral and celebratory, lay behind Dolce & Gabbana's designs for spring 2008, which *Vogue*'s Sarah Mower said had 'ticked all the boxes of trend without wavering from their own heartland for a second'. In a collection Mower deemed 'a virtuoso performance that showed them at their very best', the designers invited ten young graduate artists from the Accademia di Brera in Milan to take bolts of silk tulle and organza and paint them like canvas, with the resulting, completely unique fabrics whipped into raw-edged dresses in loosely 1950s silhouettes. The results were sensational, adding both artistic gravitas and exuberant whimsicality to the perfected craft of the Dolce & Gabbana metier. It was *haute couture* in all but name, being the finest expression yet of Dolce & Gabbana's unique, handcrafted beauty and, like *haute couture*, available only to order.

'Everything is possible because, in one second, everything can change.'

DOMENICO DOLCE

In a metallic leather corset
dress from a collection Vogue
described as 'part Erotica-era
Madonna, part Barbarella',
model Julia Stegner strikes
a powerful pose for Regan
Cameron in 2007.

Overleaf Daria Werbowy sits
pretty for Patrick Demarchelier
in 2008, wearing a gown of
loosely swagged silk hand-
painted by young artists from
Milan's Accademia di Brera.

'IT'S ABOUT
THE CONCEPT.
IT'S NOT JUST
A DRESS, IT'S A
DREAM — THE
DOLCE DREAM.'

DOLCE & GABBANA

'Matching the opposites is the essence of our whole work and the secret behind that bit of irony we love to put into everything we do', Stefano Gabbana once told *Vogue*, and hence the following season's collection was different again. It was entitled *Pigiama Barocco*, though these were not indoor pyjamas. Paired with swinging crystal-embedded cocktail bags and nestled amongst more traditional high-glamour cocktail dresses, the designers here proposed a new favoured silhouette for louche eveningwear, a dress code they still believe in as they continue issuing pairs of silk pyjamas as an option for guests attending their exclusive private parties held in venues from Hollywood to Cannes.

However, one aspect had been seen consistently through the designer's output as the 2000s drew to a close: there was more and more eveningwear on the Dolce & Gabbana catwalk, with daywear a component more likely to be found at D&G. Creatures of the night were celebrated in the most exotic way for autumn/winter 2009, a collection that saw the designers take on the legacy of legendary Italian couturier Elsa Schiaparelli. Shown during the same week that the designers were hosting a party for the *Extreme Beauty in Vogue* book, and the exhibition of the same name at Milan's Palazzo della Ragione, Dolce & Gabbana's own surrealist experiment took Schiaparelli's famed balloon sleeve and mixed it with ever more extreme elements, from eye-popping Op Art mirror disc embellishment to designs in shocking pink goat fur. For *Vogue*, the look was the perfect pick for pop's new surrealist queen, Lady Gaga, who smouldered like a modern-day Marilyn in a black lace dress with exploding tulle at the shoulder.

Proving their endless appeal to performers (especially the more provocative ones), Lady Gaga dons a lace and silk-tulle form-fitting dress for photographer Josh Olins' portrait for Vogue in 2009.

Overleaf Pyjamas for evening are a keynote for Dolce & Gabbana. In 2009 Terry Tsiolis photographed model Anna Selezneva in the louche chic of a Barolo-hued silk satin pair (left). The designers' autumn/winter 2009's tribute to designer Elsa Schiaparelli and the surrealists of the early 20th century sees Sasha Pivovarova don a balloon-sleeved silk Mikado jacket and charm necklace (right) for Patrick Demarchelier.

I love Dolce & Gabbana . . . I love the crazy, more eccentric stuff.

LADY GAGA

From the earliest part of their shared career, Gabbana had pressed Dolce to examine and explore the subtleties and hidden codes and of Domenico's homeland, Sicily, to establish a solid and expressive foundation from which to take their frequent flights of fancy. They have continued to make the heart of the brand innately Sicilian. Speaking to American *Vogue* in 2000, Gabbana explained, 'Sicilian style for me is about a passion for life. It's about one colour – black – that then absorbs all the other stronger colours. Domenico has that passion for life inside him.' For his part, Dolce offered poetically to *Vogue Italia* in 2005: 'I rediscovered, thanks to Stefano, my land that I had left to arrive in Milan, a little overwhelmed, tired of excess tradition, the claustrophobic weight of a vast past. The ceramics of Caltagirone, a crochet curtain that sways in the wind, candies like colourful architecture, prickly pears, agaves, palms. A dreamlike Sicily, far away, full of symbols and suggestion, which are hidden and not given. Never.'

For spring/summer 2010, with a collection titled *A Sicilian Way of Life*, Gabbana's fascination for Sicilian black met with Dolce's own childhood memories of life at his father's tailors where, as he had asserted to American *Vogue* in 1991, 'By the age of six or seven, I was able to chalk up, baste, and sew a man's jacket. By ten, I was a specialist in men's pants.' Four decades of experience expressed itself in masterfully crafted suits of black satin; these were set against the more familiar house favourites of black lace shifts and corsets, and interspersed with lighter looks in white broderie anglaise. Symbolising the rugged sensuality of the island and combining it with the pure sartorial wit of Dolce & Gabbana also came a corseted bodice hewn from sackcloth hessian, a design into which *Vogue* poured a sultry Kate Moss, in a brooding shot by Willy Vanderperre.

'Sicily inspires us in everything we do. It is the heart and passion of this company.'

STEFANO GABBANA

By autumn 2010, Dolce & Gabbana had really come back to their homeland. Against a powerful and emotional background video showing the Dolce & Gabbana atelier at work – with Domenico tacking the lines of a lapel and Stefano sculpting sensuous dresses in black macramé, both surrounded by their doting design team in white coats – the show opened with a sextet of the ultimate Dolce & Gabbana garment: black double-breasted men's jackets carved and padded to a full feminine curve.

From here came forth an immaculate collection of house hit after house hit in leopard spot, polka dot, lingerie lace, grey flannel and flecks of gold, free of all gimmickry. As Sarah Mower of American *Vogue* put succinctly: 'Simply, yet movingly, they showed their classics, and how they make them.' The show closed with a finale of 85 models re-emerging in the opening display of black jacket over black briefs, an army of beautiful and beautifully different Dolce & Gabbana women that had much of the audience (and probably some of the thousands watching the show streamed live online) in tears.

The designers had put a perfect end to their quarter century and then, again, they set about 'matching the opposites'. If the previous collection had bathed in a dark and dreamy melancholia that captured the Sicilian widow of their dreams, for the following spring Dolce & Gabbana were to purify with an almost entirely white collection. The materials were emptied from an imagined *cassone*, a trousseau given to a bride filled with all the items needed to begin a newly married life.

An image of innocence and purity, photographed in 2013 by Venetia Scott in the beautiful country garden of Great Dixter, English rose Georgia May Jagger is a chaste beauty in a white lace dress with high neckline.

Overleaf *Leopard print is a house staple, never far from the Dolce & Gabbana rack or runway. From the autumn/ winter 2005 collection the designers described as 'La Dolce Vita meets swinging London', model Behati Prinsloo brings a sense of Sixties chic to a printed chiffon dress (left) for photographer Paolo Roversi. Model Patricia van der Vliet gives a cool edge to the traditional craftsmanship of a white lace tunic (right) from the spring/summer 2010 collection entitled A Sicilian Way of Life. Photograph by Mario Testino.*

'To me, flowers are happiness.'

STEFANO GABBANA

From here were borrowed the broderie tablecloth edges, billowing, curtain-like tulles and of course a heavy dosage of wedding-night lingerie. A little digging revealed the subversion behind the seeming innocence, for the story of the woman they envisaged was that she was a southern (Italian) belle who had run away from the wedding, taking her trousseau with her. By the time the runaway bride reached the pages of *Vogue* in May, she was as far away as Africa where Tim Walker captured model Agyness Deyn hitching up a tablecloth skirt in an abandoned sand-filled house in the desert with only a cheetah for company. By June the runaway bride (now Raquel Zimmermann) was cheerful in D&G cherry print, lounging at a villa in Miami. Quite the great escape.

Shot by Tim Walker in Kolmanskop, a forgotten, sand-covered ghost town deep in the Namib desert, Agyness Deyn makes acquaintance with a cheetah in a lace-edged brocade skirt and cotton bra and knickers from the headily romantic Sicilian Sensuality collection for spring/summer 2011.

For Dolce & Gabbana, autumn/winter 2011 was the return of rock and roll: Teddy boys and glam rockers were the men from whom their woman borrowed a new set of suits for the season. She was once again a performer, in sequins and star-printed chiffon or sprinkled with musical note motifs. Citing the androgynous and elfin Janelle Monáe and the, well, androgynous and elfin David Bowie, the collection was about music's ability to encompass gender fluidity and was a new way for the designers to display masculine tailoring for women. It also celebrated music itself. This has been a constant source of inspiration for Dolce and Gabbana, from their first nightclub rendezvous to the opening chords of the Intermezzo from Mascagni's *Cavalleria Rusticana*, which open almost every Dolce & Gabbana show, to stars such as Whitney Houston and Kylie Minogue who have picked Dolce & Gabbana to costume their tours and stage performances. In 1996 Dolce and Gabbana even released a hard trance single entitled 'D&G Music'.

Encouraging one another's outside interests as individuals has invariably benefitted Dolce & Gabbana the collective. Following his publication of *Campioni*, a book of photographic portraits of prominent Italian footballers, published in 2012 Domenico Dolce felt confident enough to take over the shooting of Dolce & Gabbana's

advertising campaigns. He joined an illustrious list of photographers including Steven Meisel, Helmut Newton and Mario Sorrenti. The move was credited by Stefano Gabbana as one of several astute creative decisions that would reposition the company's expenditure in order to weather the wake of the 2008 financial crash. The spring/summer 2013 campaign starred Bianca Balti, Monica Bellucci and Bianca Brandolini d'Adda surrounded by hordes of male admirers on a beach in Taormina. Again, it was Gabbana who had encouraged Dolce to explore this passion. 'The most difficult thing, during these years, is explaining what it is we really want from the pictures – what message it is we want to give the audience', Gabbana explained. 'We decide the models and we decide the music and we do the fittings. So we know exactly what we want to communicate to people. And so in the end, why not?' The risk paid off, and Dolce acted as his house's own photographer for six campaigns before handing over to Franco Pagetti, the acclaimed Italian war photographer.

Taking its lead from the mainline collection's runaway bride theme, spring/summer 2011's D&G collection was a cornucopia of escapist prints. Photographed by Josh Olins, Raquel Zimmermann sizzles in a cotton bikini bandeau and pencil skirt in popping cherry print.

***Overleaf** With Domenico Dolce shooting the spring/summer 2013 advertising campaign and Stefano Gabbana styling it, the designers showed the completeness of their vision from first sketch to point-of-sale. Starring Monica Bellucci and a supporting cast drawn from the towns and villages of Sicily, the campaign, shot on location, was inspired by Visconti's 1948 film* La Terra Trema *following the trials and tribulations of a group of Sicilian fishermen.*

W hilst Dolce has taken care of Dolce & Gabbana's seasonal output of imagery, Gabbana is in his own element on social media. An Instagram addict, Gabbana spearheads the brand's outreach into the global online community, with over 900,000 followers for his personal account alone. His celebration of new media informed the feather-ruffling decision to fill the front row of the spring/summer 2010 show with a host of the supposedly establishment-threatening new breed of bloggers in places usually reserved for the print-based elite. For the spring/summer 2016 show, models even greeted the end of the catwalk with a selfie instead of a pose for the waiting cameras in front of them.

Today the casting of models for shows and advertising campaigns is heavily influenced by their social media following and the significant promotional aspect that brings. Dolce & Gabbana took this one step further for autumn/winter 2017 womens and menswear collections.

DOLCE & GABBANA

The brand adopted a coterie of social media sensations, comprised of debutant A-list offspring, YouTube hosts followed by millions and teenage pop stars, and christened them #DGMillennials. Now they took to the Dolce & Gabbana catwalk whose front row they had graced the previous season.

As a partnership, it is perhaps the permanent presence of an ally that has helped Dolce and Gabbana survive the inevitable criticism that their profile has brought them over the years, from a bad reception of a catwalk collection (which the pair say they can sense from their brief walk onto the runway afterwards and confirm to one another with a look), to misadventures – accusations thereof – generated off the catwalk. In late 2009, as Italy reeled from the global financial crisis, the designers and several senior executives were charged with alleged tax evasion. After an investigation the previous year Italy's fiscal authorities claimed a total of 416 million euros was owed, and at one point suggested fines of up to 800 million euros. The case, which stemmed from the sale in 2004 of both Dolce & Gabbana and D&G to a holding company in Luxembourg, was vehemently denied by the two men. It would dog them for five fraught years thanks in part to the complexity of Italy's legal system. In October 2014 Italy's highest court – the Corte di Cassazione – ruled that there had never been any legal grounds for the case in the first place. 'We were certain!' said Gabbana on social media, adding: 'We are honest people.'

The pair could be forgiven if they wished to wash their hands of the trials and tribulations that came with the responsibility of spearheading such a major concern. By now both fabulously wealthy, the duo could easily sell up, sit back and enjoy the spoils of a quarter of a century of work. The pair were not finished though; there was another story to be added.

Stefano Gabbana and Domenico Dolce pose in an explosion of ticker tape for photographer Terry Richardson in a celebratory portrait for Vogue marking the 25th anniversary of Dolce & Gabbana, April 2011.

'CLOTHES WITH SUCH A STRONG
PERSONALITY THAT WHOEVER
SEES THEM CAN INSTANTLY SAY
WITHOUT A SHADOW OF A DOUBT:
THIS IS A DOLCE & GABBANA.'

DOMENICO DOLCE

HIGHER AND HIGHER

The most recent advance of the Dolce & Gabbana empire began with what appeared to many as a retreat. In September 2011, immediately after the showing of the spring/summer 2012 D&G show, the designers disclosed it would be the last ever for the 17-year-old, $5300-million-turnover second line, one making up over 40% of the firm's wholesale revenues. D&G's 68 standalone stores were to be incorporated into the Dolce & Gabbana network and the famous D&G logo would remain, but those letters no longer represented a brand of their own. Many retailers – especially those that only offered the second brand – were left scratching their heads: why on earth would the designers (who had reassumed control of D&G from its licensee in 2007) ever consider closing such a money-spinner?

Just ahead of her Oscar win the following February, Jennifer Lawrence appears on the cover of the November issue of Vogue in a lace dress over a satin body taken from Dolce & Gabbana's autumn/ winter 2012 collection, the first since the closure of the D&G line. Photograph by Alasdair McLellan.

Dolce & Gabbana said in a statement: 'To us, it's going back to when we began our adventure; full of ideas. We have a lot of new projects to start in the same way as many years ago when D&G was born. This is our new reality and we are extremely happy about it.' Backstage, after that final show, the designers seemed liberated by their decision. Gabbana said: 'In the future we want to work to one style … and it's time to sketch just one collection because when we die we would love to leave one label recognisable to the world'. Dolce added: 'We don't want to be the richest men in the cemetery'. In September 2011, a new fine jewellery line was launched with a collection incorporating antique and religious charms, and it was an affirmation of Dolce & Gabbana's commitment to craftsmanship and tradition.

By early 2012, in total secrecy, a new collection was being worked on, one that would evolve Dolce & Gabbana as a fashion house in its most complete sense, fulfilling the designers' longest-held dream and one that now had a name: Alta Moda, the Italian translation of 'haute couture'. The project was to establish for Dolce & Gabbana, at its top level, an haute couture house, but one unbound by the rules (and limitations) of the traditional, Paris-defined notions of the form.

VOGUE

NOV
£4.10

Vogue's
100
The best places
to shop online

TREND REPORT
Which shoe
are you?

**FACES
OF NOW**
London's
cool kids

*Autumn
beauty update*
Blockbuster scents and
out-there make-up

JENNIFER
LAWRENCE
Style and
substance

Shine!
**BRILLIANT
NEW PARTY
PIECES**

*Chop
and
change*
How to
cut your
own hair

'OUR DREAM IS TO CREATE A STYLE WHICH IS TIMELESS.'

DOMENICO DOLCE

Before the first show there were reasons to suspect that this project might well turn out to be an expensive self-indulgence. Haute couture itself had been in decline for decades. From a peak of more than 100 recognised Parisian *maisons de couture* in the late 1940s the Paris schedule now comprised barely 20. The 1970s rise of ready-to-wear – a phenomenon of which Dolce & Gabbana had been a beneficiary – had rendered the notion of a top-tier of fashion houses providing entirely bespoke handmade clothing practically redundant. The Paris couture shows functioned as much to create confections for the press as for clients (of whom most houses could number fewer than 100); they acted as loss-leading marketing exercises to emphasise the elevated status of those houses that still had the resources to support them. So what could Dolce & Gabbana add to the 150-year-old genre?

Their answer was revealed that July – immediately after the Paris couture shows – in the hilly Sicilian coastal resort town of Taormina. Under the direction of Cornelia 'Coco' Brandolini d'Adda – a scion of both the Agnelli family and Lombardian aristocracy – who was retained by Dolce & Gabbana as the 'chief ambassador' of Alta Moda, a guest list of 80 potential clients was invited to the first presentation. They came from Russia, Qatar, the UK, China, the US, and indeed anywhere where Brandolini and her team had surmised there lived a woman who was either so committed to Dolce & Gabbana (or more broadly to haute couture) that she might want to take part. As this was the first ever presentation of the collection – and a leap in the dark for its audience – Dolce & Gabbana contributed to their invitees' travel and accommodation expenses, though this incentive would not long remain necessary.

Previous page Damaris Goddrie and Frederikke Sofie form a perfect pair in silk-satin pyjamas of painterly rose print on a rich blue ground, photographed by Tyrone Lebon in 2016.

'We feel a special bond with Sicily and its people.'

STEFANO GABBANA

From the start, it was clear that this would be like no other couture show. Rather than the usual quick in-and-out of a half-an-hour presentation, Dolce & Gabbana's Alta Moda showing was scheduled to last two days. On the first, guests were invited to a warm-up for the immersion into Italian culture to come: a performance of the Sicilian composer Vincenzo Bellini's opera *Norma* in Taormina's Roman amphitheatre. Afterwards, there was a feast on a hillside that overlooked the glow of Mount Etna and the thunderclap of a specially commissioned firework display. On day two – after a morning of leisure and the chance to digest the first in what would become a series of specially commissioned books by *Vogue Italia*'s Art Director Luca Stoppini – came the collection.

Guests entered past a mise-en-scène of models wearing sheer lace gowns whose skirts were boned to an enormous diameter. In the grand courtyard of the monastery of San Domenico, as guests settled on scattered sofas and piles of cushions, it became apparent that this was so much more than a fashion show. There were celebrities – friends of the house such as Scarlett Johansson and Monica Bellucci – and there was press – journalists from three European newspapers and representatives from around ten international editions of *Vogue*. But apart from Dolce & Gabbana's own, there were no photographers. The journalists had been invited on the proviso that they did not reveal the names of any clients without their express permission – and everybody was asked not to share any photographs of the clothes on social media. *Vogue*'s editors were to be offered the opportunity to shoot a very small selection of looks should they so desire. Why all the (relative) confidentiality? 'Because no client wants to see a picture of her dress – her unique, one-off dress – in the newspaper,' said Gabbana.

One-by-one, seventy-three designs then came crunching sedately down the gravel, each perfectly rendered in superlative fabrics, often woven through with real gold thread, such as silk organdie crépon, brocade and astoundingly detailed lace. Travelling through a section of tailored daywear with lace overlaid, the show climaxed with a series of hand-painted ballgowns echoing Claudia Cardinale's room-transfixers in *The Leopard*. Immaculate chignons were accented by vintage hats, reworked and embellished, or with garlands of blossom. Some extraordinary pieces of Alta Gioielleria, their fine jewellery line, including gold starburst pendants strung on black velvet ribbon and huge baroque gold and ruby earrings, were made to complement various pieces. Understandably in awe, *Vogue Italia* described the collection as 'masterpieces made to be interpreted by extraordinary women'.

Despite the heat (several guests fainted during the weekend), it was an intensely romantic, utterly immersive show. Afterwards guests were invited to view the collection and consider purchase, assured only one of each would ever be made. Certain clients ordered several pieces and many others one or two, and by the end of the evening these privileged women, their swains and retinue, plus the designers and a selection of the fashion faithful were all dancing in a Taormina cypress grove. For all of its extravagance, here Dolce & Gabbana were in fact showing their own fashion pragmatism. One of the many reasons cited for the demise of traditional haute couture, which had survived several recessions, was a move to more casual living. An informal world of comfortable sneakers and greater democracy had done away with occasion dressing, elaborate balls and debutantes; so, here Dolce & Gabbana provided not only outrageously opulent fashion, but also an event at which to wear it. From here, the shows would grow only more elaborate in setting and execution, giving potential clients a dream to buy into.

For autumn/winter 2012's inaugural Alta Moda collection, Boo George photographed model Karlina Caune as the chatelaine of a golden country estate. Here, she wears a hand-painted silk-organdie crépon dress with a straw hat adorned with velvet roses.

Overleaf *In a pastoral setting, Boo George gives the Dolce & Gabbana leading lady the air of a Marie Antoinette-style shepherdess in further pieces from the 2012 Alta Moda collection – a hand-painted organza dress with pannier petticoat and silk organdie headpiece.*

'No matter how old you are, you never stop dreaming, so why would you when it comes to clothes?'

STEFANO GABBANA

The second show, held in Milan in January 2013, showed clients the extent to which Dolce & Gabbana had committed their resources to this tilt at greatness. The collection was presented in the new Alta Moda *salone*, a large recently purchased suite of several floors just behind Via della Spiga. On its roof – after some wrangling with Milan's planning authorities – they had built an extra floor clad in glass in which to entertain guests after the collection, as well as to present their now established Alta Gioielleria collection of fine jewellery. The idea, it seemed, was to create a hermetically sealed luxury environment in which to seduce – with great panache – the by now 100-strong list of invited clients and potential clients.

A very few of them – the most committed – were also given the chance to tour one of the Alta Moda ateliers. The largest of these, at a secret Milan address, employs several scores of technicians – who wear black lace collars over the traditional white lab coats to work – over four floors. This is where new fabrics are developed, the vintage fabrics that are incorporated into certain looks each season are reworked, and all of the embroidery and other detailing is perfected. Typically each dress takes five seamstresses four to five days from start to finish. Then there is another, entirely separate tailoring atelier, which was starting to share some resources with menswear, for a number of one-off commissions. The main atelier contained the specially made mannequins that are constructed for each new client, to conform exactly to their measurements for fitting and checks between appointments. It is run by a *première* (head dressmaker) with 22 years' experience working for the company. The staff working below her, said Gabbana, 'are the ones who have been with us forever, the best'.

Thematically, the second Alta Moda presentation explored the idea of uniting fashion and context, with the parade of sumptuous looks featuring embellishments based on curlicued mouldings on the walls of the newly refurbished Via Senato salon. Tailoring – just a few pieces – featured inside-out inverted stitching to hint at the architecture of canvas and panel behind the façade. The more

extravagantly grandiose pieces included tulle gowns peppered with shards of coral and jewels. The last look was accessorised with a crown and a pair of kitten heels wrought of solid gold and lined in quilted satin. Apparently, they sold.

From here, Alta Moda would stage its elaborate presentations, season by season, all over Italy, celebrating the inspiration that each region had provided to the house. The summer 2013 host locale was Venice, with a magnificent show held in the salon of the Palazzo Barbaro. The collection featured lace cut into harlequin panels and climaxed with ballgowns painted with homages to Canaletto and the Venetian cityscape. It featured a 700-piece dress that had taken a total of three months to complete. Lisa Armstrong of *The Daily Telegraph* concluded, 'This was certainly the best show of couture week, which is quite a feat considering they've only been making couture for three seasons.' That evening, Dolce & Gabbana had arranged a masked ball for clients to dance anonymously in Alta Moda until dawn.

Following the January 2014 spring/summer collection back in Milan – which featured dresses embellished with decorations drawn from flowers painted by artists including Van Gogh, Renoir, Manet and Klimt – that summer 200 guests, including the members of one Middle Eastern royal family and the wife and daughters of one former head of state, were invited to Capri. Of the presentation Domenico Dolce said: 'It's about this place, Capri: our ultimate fantasy version of it … as well as being about the clothes. In Alta Moda we try and communicate a total feeling, a complete emotion in the show.' It was held near dusk on a picturesque outcrop in the shadow of the Faraglioni rocks, which had also provided the backdrop for David Gandy in the Light Blue fragrance campaign shot so memorably by Mario Testino. The models arrived around the headland on ribbon-strewn boats, stepped onto a jetty and then moved on into the crowd.

Shot for Vogue *by Boo George in Capri (where the autumn/ winter 2014 collection had been shown that July), model Kinga Rajak sports a hand-painted map of the glamorous island made into a sculptural and feminine dress.*

The collection featured a contrast between decadently rendered leisurewear – shaved bustier-bikinis, chinchilla t-shirts, bloomers and moonboots – and full-skirted, deckchair-stripe, fantasy frocks topped by hand-embroidered parasols sprinkled with gemstones. Fur-trimmed tweed jackets, sheath dresses in vintage brocades from the 1950s and 1960s, drop-waisted skirts with the outline of the Capri coastline etched in sequins, and one dress with hidden integrated miniature cymbals that tinkled as the wearer walked were a few of the other standout looks. The climax of the show saw yet another boat cut across the sea, with a veiled model wearing a full-skirted wedding dress at its prow like a figurehead and as the sun slipped below the horizon there was a 20-minute firework extravaganza.

As had become form for the spring/summer collections, the show the following January was held in Milan. The venue, however, was both new and a coup. The previous November the designers decided to theme their collection around the history of ballet and opera at La Scala, Milan's great eighteenth-century opera house. When they approached Alexander Pereira, La Scala's newly appointed CEO and artistic director, to obtain permission Dolce also threw in a supplemental request: might they hold their show there, too? This seemed the stuff of fantasy: La Scala had never opened its heavy wooden doors to Milan's fashion industry before. But, said Dolce, 'if I hadn't asked the question, it would have kept bothering me.' Pereira said yes. Gabbana said that the designers were both elated and flabbergasted: 'Afterward, I was trying to keep a straight face, but in the car home I was screaming. For us to be here is amazing – like touching the sky with your finger.'

'It's the fashion system's fault that no one tells a story today' offered Stefano Gabbana at the autumn/winter 2015 Alta Moda collection shown in the designers' own properties in Portofino on the Ligurian coast. In response came a fantastical collection inspired by Homer, Dante and Shakespeare, including these two full-skirted gowns, in vivid silk-screened prints of watermelons and macaws, with crystal corseted bustiers.

The spring/summer 2015 show was held in the ornate marble galleria that flanks the main auditorium. By now there were nearly 200 clients on the Alta Moda roster – many of them now set-in-stone regulars, whose husbands and partners had themselves become clients of the slowly emerging menswear equivalent. The collection featured a greater emphasis than previously on day-wear: there were 15 black dresses in wool and crêpe cut to exactingly precise variations of the

designer's core repertoire of proportion and silhouette. This almost straightforward section, however, was enveloped in romance. The show opened and closed with world-renowned ballet dancer Roberto Bolle and six coral-tulle-clad dancers from La Scala's academy dancing, beautifully, down the parquet catwalk. Bolero jackets, opera cloaks and closely fitted matador trousers marched between whooshes of rustling vintage jacquard organza. Vintage ballet posters appeared as if plastered billboard-style, first in sequinned shift tops and then in hand-screened sheets of silk on huge gowns skirted in scarlet, black or white tulle. Afterwards, Gabbana remarked: 'This is about experimentation and about training. Every season we move and every season the quality improves. Alta Moda has taught us both to move with more freedom. OK, we have to think about the market. But we do not care so much about that now. Through Alta Moda we have become more confident to express ourselves.'

Autumn/winter 2015 saw the first Alta Sartoria – couture tailoring for men – presentation to be held alongside those for Alta Moda and Alta Gioielleria, completing an all-encompassing project later labelled Alte Artigianalità. The venue was Portofino, where both Dolce and Gabbana own exclusive nearby mansions clinging to the rocks. Literally presenting the shows in their own back yard – 'Stefano's house is the showroom, my house is a backstage for the models' Dolce told Vogue.com – there was of course nothing else domestic about it. The fabulous Alta Moda show, which drew on the fantastical literature of Homer, Dante, Shakespeare and Lewis Carroll, saw hand-printed silks adorn skirts (now more softly built in volume with layers of silk petticoats) that graced models sweeping through arches of fresh flowers. The following evening's debut Alta Sartoria show featured everything a gentleman could need to dress for an evening of luxury, from velvet tuxedos embroidered exquisitely with exotic birds in the Japanese style to the pyjamas to wake up in the next day.

'CLOTHES FOR
WOMEN WHO
WANTED TO
FEEL LIKE A
PAPAL NUNCIO.'

THE NEW YORKER

By the spring/summer 2016 Alta Moda collection, presented the day after the Alta Sartoria collection for men and set on the very stage of La Scala, Dolce & Gabbana returned to a core design ethos whereby a woman as well as an Italian context became the focus. The 88-look collection described by International *Vogue* Editor Suzy Menkes as an 'aria of excellence', looked to one of Italy's famed mid-twentieth-century couturiers: Elvira Leonardi Bouyeure, known more commonly as Biki. The step-granddaughter of Giacomo Puccini and a friend of Maria Callas, Biki's life was profoundly intertwined with events at La Scala. The collection honoured this with an operatic tribute that combined embroideries showing vintage programmes for Puccini's masterpieces *Tosca*, *Turandot* and *Madama Butterfly* and Biki's own couture sketches. Alta Gioielleria pieces included both prima-donna coronets and witty winks to couture itself in the form of platinum tape-measure necklaces.

I t is important to stress that Dolce & Gabbana's Alte Artigianalità has not superseded the impact of the ready-to-wear collections, which remain, to a global audience and international fashion press, the more publicity-driven events, streamed live over the internet. Apart from the autumn/winter 2016 show that took place in public on the cobbled streets of Naples, Alte Artigianalità is much more protective of the imagery disseminated from its shows because of its aim of retaining the unique exclusivity of garments for its customers.

The relationship between the two levels of output is rich and symbiotic. At its inauguration, Alte Artigianalità's immediate impact on ready-to-wear was to make the designers assess the core philosophy of the Dolce & Gabbana brand, and it led to their giving the collections for both men and women a defined focus on the characters of Sicily, the capital of the Dolce & Gabbana empire.

As it developed, the Alte Artigianalità project served to raise both the standards and the profile of Dolce & Gabbana ready-to-wear. The continuing high level of commitment in craft and design can be seen in the subtle perfection of a tailored cashmere skirt suit from the spring/summer 2013 collection photographed on model Drake Burnette by Josh Olins.

Overleaf *In January 2016, Dolce & Gabbana launched a range aimed at the Muslim market. 'The garments, while engineered for modesty, have all the flair of any other Dolce & Gabbana collection', said Vogue. Here, an abaya and hijab ensemble in a print scattered with daisies is completed with a patchworked snakeskin handbag and crystal-embellished 'Margherite' sunglasses.*

'A RANGE ... ALL
DEMONSTRATING
THE DRAMATIC
FEMININITY THAT
THE BRAND
HAS BUILT ITS
NAME ON.'

VOGUE

NOV
£3.99

Bond
bombshell
Léa
Seydoux

Ultimate
**BEAUTY
SHORTCUTS**

**HANGING
OUT WITH
LIV TYLER**

The
extraordinary
world of
**KARL
LAGERFELD**

**A WINTER
WEEKEND
WARDROBE**

New
codes
of cool

NEWSFLASH
The woman
at the top of
British media

Autumn
style

The rich and multi-layered historical anthropology of Sicily inspired collections drawing on ever-more hidden, perhaps esoteric aspects, peaking with the autumn/winter 2014 look at the island's Norman invasion. This was followed by spring/summer 2015 and men's and women's shows taking a broad Spanish theme, inspired by the Spanish command of Sicily from 1516–1713. These collections enabled Dolce & Gabbana to explore aspects of their domestic culture and relate them to ever more foreign contexts. This passion for inclusivity has personal resonance for Dolce & Gabbana as well as displaying a shrewd business approach for a continually growing international brand. It has led to various outreaches into growing markets such as a showing of their Alta Moda and Alta Sartoria collections in Hong Kong in 2016 and the launch the same year of a collection of printed hijabs and abayas aimed at its Muslim clientele.

Actress Léa Seydoux exudes elegance and femininity in a ruched tulle sheath dress emblazoned with an exaggerated rose appliqué taken from the autumn/winter 2015 Viva la Mamma collection. Photograph by Craig McDean.

Overleaf *An angelic host of models, Adriana Lima, Lais Ribeiro, Candice Swanepoel and Elsa Hosk, sweep the floor in full, hand-painted organza skirts from the autumn/winter 2014 Alta Moda collection. Photograph by Patrick Demarchelier.*

The Alte Artigianalità project, Dolce explains, 'has taught us a lot: to pay attention to the details and to make the message more focused. To define the essence.' Its grand tour of Italy has served Dolce & Gabbana's aim of building a house with a true design philosophy at its heart, taking an original inspiration to new heights and providing perfect excuses for the happy celebration that is essential to both the men and the brand. Italy and its endless treasures and pleasures are likely to offer decades of inspiration to come: 'We are lucky to have such beauty', says Dolce, 'Napoli, Roma, Venezia, Parma, Bologna … The wine, the pasta, the oil … Italy has the best qualities and you wake up to a culture of beauty'. In paying tribute to this beauty, Dolce and Gabbana have created a serious body of work, while still having the ability to sprinkle their designs with the whimsy and less-complicated charms that will seduce a younger customer whom they hope will grow in sophistication with them. And with that a new generation of the Dolce & Gabbana family is born.

Index

Page numbers in *italic* refer to illustrations

References

Carugati, Decio G. *20 Years of Dolce & Gabbana for Men* Mondadori Electa, 2010

Mower, Sarah *20 Years: Dolce & Gabbana* Five Continents Editions, 2005

Rossellini, Isabella *10 Years of Dolce & Gabbana* Abbeville Press, 1996

Sozzani, Franca *Dolce & Gabbana: Fashion Memoir* Thames & Hudson, 1998

Stanfill, Sonnett *The Glamour of Italian Fashion Since 1945* V&A Publishing, 2014

Wiederin, Alex *Dolce and Gabbana: Diamonds and Pearls* Mondadori Electa, 2007

Picture credits

Acknowledgements

The authors would like to thank Alexandra Shulman for setting this book in motion. Thanks also to Simona Baroni, Andrea Caravita and Matteo Caoduro at Dolce & Gabbana as well as to Brett Croft and Carole Dumoulin at Condé Nast. Thanks also go to Drusilla Beyfus, Harriet Wilson and Jaime Perlman for their generosity, guidance and wisdom. And, finally, thanks to Domenico Dolce and Stefano Gabbana for their encouragement and openness – and all those beautiful shows.

Publishing Consultant Jane O'Shea
Creative Director Helen Lewis
Series Editor Sarah Mitchell
Series Designer Nicola Ellis
Designer Gemma Hayden
Production Director Vincent Smith
Production Controller Nikolaus Ginelli

For *Vogue*:
Commissioning Editor Harriet Wilson
Picture Researcher Carole Dumoulin

First published in 2017 by
Quadrille Publishing Limited
Pentagon House
52-54 Southwark Street
London SE1 1UN
www.quadrille.com

Reprinted in 2019
10 9 8 7 6 5 4 3 2

Text copyright © 2017 Condé Nast
Publications Limited
Vogue Regd TM is owned by the Condé
Nast Publications Ltd and is used under
licence from it. All rights reserved.

Design and layout © 2017 Quadrille
Publishing Limited

Quadrille is an imprint of Hardie Grant
www.hardiegrant.com

Cataloguing in Publication Data: a
catalogue record for this book is
available from the British Library.

ISBN 978 184949 972 9

Printed in China